GREAT CITIES
of the
WORLD

First published in Australia in 2011 by Young Reed
an imprint of New Holland Publishers (Australia) Pty Ltd
Sydney • Auckland • London • Cape Town
www.newholland.com.au

1/66 Gibbes Street Chatswood NSW 2067 Australia
218 Lake Road Northcote Auckland New Zealand
86 Edgware Road London W2 2EA United Kingdom
80 McKenzie Street Cape Town 8001 South Africa

A record of this book is available at the National Library of Australia

ISBN: 9781921580000 (hbk.)

Publisher: Diane Jardine
Publishing manager: Lliane Clarke
Senior editor: Mary Trewby
Design: Amanda Tarlau
Production manager: Olga Dementiev
Printer: Toppan Leefung Printing Limited

Picture Credits

Abbreviations: t = top, b = bottom, l = left, r = right, c = centre, m = main picture

Abxbay 16c; **Adam.J.W.C.** 21c; **José-Manuel Benito** 8t; **Ian Boxall** 8m, 32cr, 32b, 33tr, 33c, 33b; **Phillip Capper** 30b, 31t, 31b; **Emily Walker** 31c; **David Schwen** 11t; **Dendodge** 10b; **Tomás Fano** 10t; **Rochelle Fernandez** 22b; **Russell Ferrett** 6c, 13t, 13b, 14t, 14b, 15tl, 15c, 17 all, 20c, 20b, 21t, 22t, 22c, 25t, 26 all, 27 all, 28 all, 29t, 29cl, 29cr, 32t, 35t, 35b, 36 all, 37 all, 38t, 38c, 38br, 39 all, 42 all, 43 all, 44 all, 45 all; **Dmitry Fironov** 34cl; **Bernard Gagnon** 33tl; **Yair Hakiai** 19b; **High Contrast** 19t; **iStockphoto** 9b, 34cr, 34b, 40t, 41b; **Brian Kell** 35cr; **Margaret & Tony Kidney** 7cl, 41t; **Siyad Ma** 29b; **Talina McKenzie** 14c; **Monsarc** 7c; **Alan Moore** 18b; **Patrick Morin** 32cl; **neajjean** 6t; **New Holland Image Library/Graeme Gillies** 20t, 25b; **Rich Niewiroski Jr** 9c; **Roboppy** 15b; **Mary Sadler** 10c, 11c, 11b; **Wolfgang Sauber** 38bl; **Shutterstock** 1, 2–3, 12t, 15tr, 16t, 16b, 23 all, 24 all, 30t, 34t, 35cl, 40c, 40b; **Wellington Sculpture Trust** 30c; **Barbara Weimer** 12bl, 12br, 13c; **Phil Whitehouse** 21b; **Paul Wilhelm** 7t; **Mark Williamson** 6–7b

Front cover iStockphoto (main), Shutterstock (bl & bc), Brian Kell (br)

GREAT CITIES
of the
WORLD

Russell Ferrett

young
reed

Contents

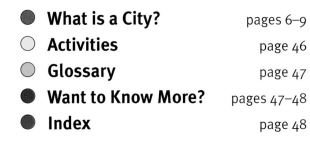

WHAT IS A CITY?

A city is a place where a large number of people live and work at jobs other than farming. Why do we like some cities and not others? Different people have different likes and dislikes, but there are some cities nearly everybody likes. These are the cities that have great variety or have something special that no other city has. Let's look at some of those cities.

Bangkok, Thailand

What about Thailand's capital, Bangkok, as a great city? It's full of lovely, friendly people and lots of noisy traffic and bustle. It also has such wonderful palaces and temples, which you can't see anywhere else in the world.

The twin cities of Niagara Falls, in Ontario, Canada, and New York state, USA, are built around the famous waterfall.

Dubai, United Arab Emirates

Dubai lies on the edge of the Arabian Desert so it's a strange place to find a large hotel shaped like a sail (left). Perhaps it's a ship of the desert. Dubai is a very modern city which has become extremely rich by selling the oil that lies beneath the desert sands.

Cambridge, England

Your parents probably hope you go to this city when you get a little older. Cambridge is one of the world's great university cities. You might like to go there for another reason. Harry Potter went there too. The university buildings were used for the making of some of the *Harry Potter* movies. How many of these films have you seen?

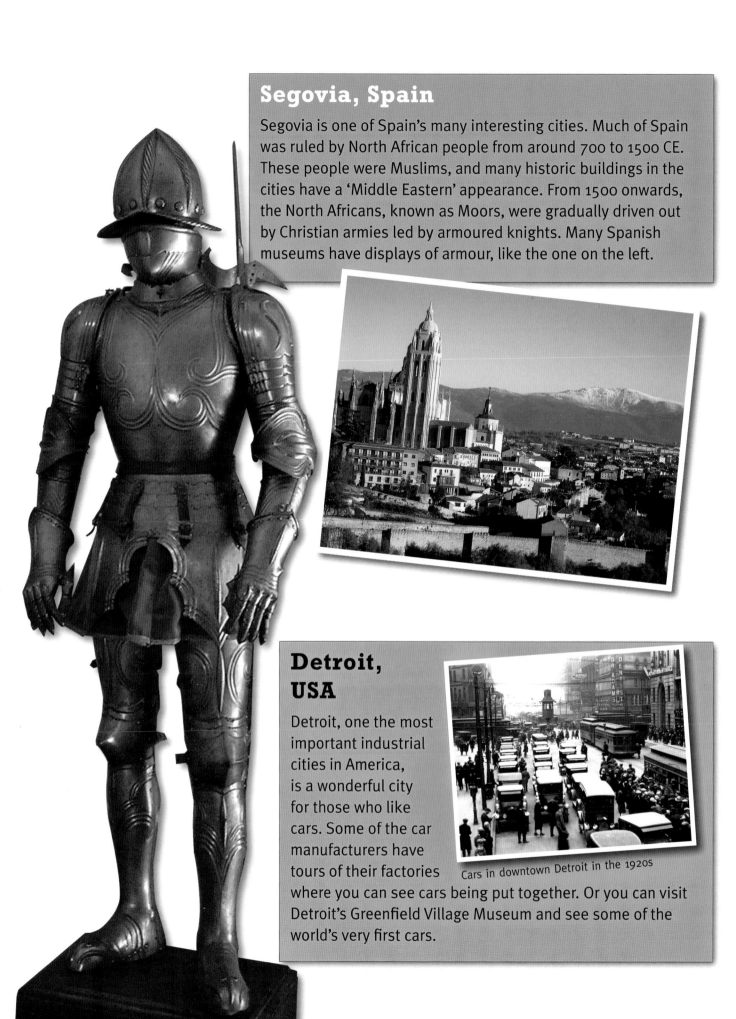

Segovia, Spain

Segovia is one of Spain's many interesting cities. Much of Spain was ruled by North African people from around 700 to 1500 CE. These people were Muslims, and many historic buildings in the cities have a 'Middle Eastern' appearance. From 1500 onwards, the North Africans, known as Moors, were gradually driven out by Christian armies led by armoured knights. Many Spanish museums have displays of armour, like the one on the left.

Detroit, USA

Detroit, one the most important industrial cities in America, is a wonderful city for those who like cars. Some of the car manufacturers have tours of their factories

Cars in downtown Detroit in the 1920s

where you can see cars being put together. Or you can visit Detroit's Greenfield Village Museum and see some of the world's very first cars.

Delhi, India

Delhi, India's capital, is a very interesting place because of its mix of Indian, British, Afghan and Persian cultures and buildings. You'd like shopping in some of the city's bustling markets where people, cattle, bicycles, carts and goods on display are all crowded together. That makes it difficult to move around.

San Francisco, USA

San Francisco is built on hills around a beautiful bay. It has many interesting places to visit. Places such as Fisherman's Wharf, Alcatraz Prison and the Golden Gate Bridge. If you want a great ride, buy a ticket on its famous cable car. Some of the hills are too steep for normal trams, so cable cars are pulled up the hills by steel ropes built into the road.

Cape Town, South Africa

Cape Town has grown a lot since it was a 'town'. It now has a population of 3,500,000. Perhaps it should change its name to Cape City! Its location right at the southern end of Africa makes it a favourite for sailors and ships sailing between Asia or Australia and Europe. They often stop here for a short break to pick up fresh supplies.

Where the World Meets
NEW YORK

One of the many things that makes New York a great city is that it is where the world's leaders in politics, finance and other important international affairs meet and make decisions that affect us all. New York was founded in 1614 by the Dutch as a fur trading post called New Amsterdam, but had its name changed to New York after it was surrendered to the British in 1664. Why do you think the British changed its name? It was the capital city of the USA for five years between 1785 and 1790.

Central Park

This famous park, 4 kilometres long (2^1/$_2$ miles) and 800 metres (^{1}/$_2$ mile) wide, is in the centre of Manhattan. It was opened in 1859 and has more than 25 million visitors a year. Why do so many people come here? Because there are lots of things to do. It has a forest, playing fields, two ice rinks, open-air theatres, a climbing area, a zoo and many gardens.

World Finance

A stock exchange is a place where shares in business companies are bought and sold. New York has the largest and most important stock exchange in the world. The New York Stock Exchange is often called 'Wall Street' because that is the name of the street on which it is located.

The United Nations

The headquarters of the United Nations (UN) is in New York City. The UN was created in 1945 at the end of World War II. One of its main functions is to try to stop wars. Nearly all of the countries in the world belong to the UN.

Skyscrapers

New York became the first city in the world to build the very tall buildings that we call skyscrapers. It is on the Atlantic Ocean coast and the main part of the city is built on an island called Manhattan. Over the centuries, it has expanded over the surrounding land.

Statue of Liberty

The Statue of Liberty stands as if on guard at the entrance to New York Harbour. The statue is hollow, 46 metres (151 feet) high and made of copper. It sits on a stone platform, which raises its overall height to 93 metres (305 feet). The statue was a gift to the United States from France in 1886 as a symbol of friendship between the two countries. Would you like to climb the 146 stairs inside the statue and peak out through its crown?

New York: Fast Facts

Country: USA
Capital city: No
Urban population: 22,000,000
Language: English
Money: US dollar

Broadway

New York has a famous theatre district where the latest plays and musical shows are performed. Many of the city's theatres, restaurants and hotels are on the street called Broadway. After a show, many people go to restaurants so the streets are often crowded, even in the middle of the night.

The Empire City
LONDON

Tower Bridge

London became great as head of the world's largest ever empire—the British Empire. Even though the empire broke up, London has continued to be a great place. You go to London to see living history such as Westminster Abbey, the Houses of Parliament, Buckingham Palace and Tower Bridge.

London's Parliament

Britain is looked upon as the home of modern democratic government. Some of the laws and democratic systems first developed in the Parliament in London are now used in many countries, including Australia, Canada, India, New Zealand, Pakistan, Sri Lanka, South Africa and the USA.

You've Got the Wrong Name

Most people know the clock on London's House of Parliament as 'Big Ben'. This is wrong. The clock's proper name is 'The Great Clock of Westminster'. The name Big Ben really belongs to the bell that chimes on the hour. Big Ben weighs nearly 14 tonnes and is 3 metres (10 feet) wide. Four smaller bells chime the quarter, half and three-quarter hours.

Is It a Rocket Ship?

No, it's a giant cucumber. This modern office building in central London is known to the locals as 'the Gherkin'. A gherkin is a common type of preserved green-coloured cucumber.

Where Time Starts

All world time is based on London time. Time is measured at a special observatory in Greenwich, a suburb of London. Time in London is said to be 'Greenwich Mean Time' (GMT). Places east of Greenwich have time ahead of Greenwich, so that Paris is an hour ahead of GMT. Farther east is Sydney, which is ten hours ahead of GMT. To the west of Greenwich places are behind GMT so that New York is five hours behind GMT and Vancouver eight hours behind.

See London Without Walking

A ride in the giant ferris wheel, the largest in the world when it opened in 2000, is an ideal way to see London in half an hour. The wheel, known as the 'London Eye', takes you 135 metres (443 feet) into the air from where you can look down on the Thames, the Houses of Parliament, Westminster Abbey and all over London. You ride in one of the 32 egg-shaped capsules that will each hold up to 25 people.

London's Sinking

Yes, London is sinking—at a rate of 1–2mm (a fraction of an inch) a year. It has been doing this since the end of the last Ice Age 10,000 years ago. When glaciers covered northern Britain, that part sank under the weight of ice and, like a giant seesaw, the southern part was lifted up. When the ice melted, the northern half rose slowly, and the southern section now slowly sinks back towards its original position. A giant dam has been built across the Thames River to stop the sea flooding back into London. Gates in the dam are normally kept open, but during storms and very high tides the gates are closed to keep the sea out.

London:
Fast Facts

Country: Britain
Capital city: Yes
Urban population: 9,000,000
Language: English
Money: Pound sterling

Most Visited
PARIS

Cathedral of Notre Dame

Paris is the most visited city in the world. More tourists visit Paris than any other city. It is known for fun, laughter, good food and having a good time. You go to Paris to walk along the Left Bank, climb the Eiffel Tower, go to a dazzling dance show, look at art exhibitions and shop for the latest fashions.

Not Going Anywhere

The Eiffel Tower was built to be a special attraction for the Paris World Fair in 1889. It was to be pulled down after 20 years. At 300 metres (1000 feet) high, it was then the world's tallest building. Many people disliked its shape and looked forward to it being pulled down. During World War I it was used to send radio signals to the battle front and became the symbol of France. It is still standing. The tower is named after its designer, Gustave Eiffel.

Is It Left or Right?

The 'Left Bank' of the River Seine that runs through Paris is home to many actors, musicians, dancers, painters and other artists—but which bank is 'Left' and which is 'Right'? If you look downstream, the way the river is flowing, the Left Bank is on your left and the Right Bank is on your right. If you look upstream, though, the Left Bank is on your right and the Right Bank is on your left! Confusing isn't it? Painters often exhibit their works out in the open along the Left Bank, hoping passers-by may buy them.

Fashion and Fun

One of the most popular theatres in Paris is the Moulin Rouge, the French for 'Red Windmill'. The theatre gets the name from the red windmill on its roof. Parisians, the name we use for people who live in Paris, love to be seen wearing the latest clothes. Indeed, the French believe that they invented fashion.

A Day at the Beach

There are no natural beaches in the middle of Paris, but you can lie on a beach just by one of the bridges across the Seine. Every summer thousands of tonnes of sand are brought in, along with palm trees and parasols, to make a sandy beach between the river and a busy road.

Cafe Society

Parisians love to sit in cafes and watch the world go by. It's almost a sport. You and your friends sit in a sidewalk cafe drinking coffee and talking. If there's nothing special to talk about, you just watch the people go by.

Paris:
Fast Facts

Country: France
Capital city: Yes
Urban population: 11,000,000
Language: French
Money: Euro

City of Canals

VENICE

Why is Venice so beautiful? It has no tree-lined streets or grassy parks, or flashy, brightly lit advertising signs or tall buildings reaching to the sky. Perhaps it's beautiful because it is so peaceful. It's quiet. There are no cars. No buses. No trucks. No trains. Just boats.

Why No Cars?

Cars, trucks and buses are not permitted in the city. Even if they were, they wouldn't fit on the bridges. Venice was built long before cars were invented. If you want to go from one part of the city to another, you can take a gondola, a water taxi or a water bus. Or you can walk. Even fire engines and ambulances are specially made boats.

Don't Run Out the Front Door!

Because if you do, you'll get wet. The front doors of most houses in Venice open onto a canal. If you are on your way to school – you go by boat. If friends come to visit you – they come by boat. The locals don't use gondolas. They're too slow. They use motor boats, which they tie up to poles near their front door.

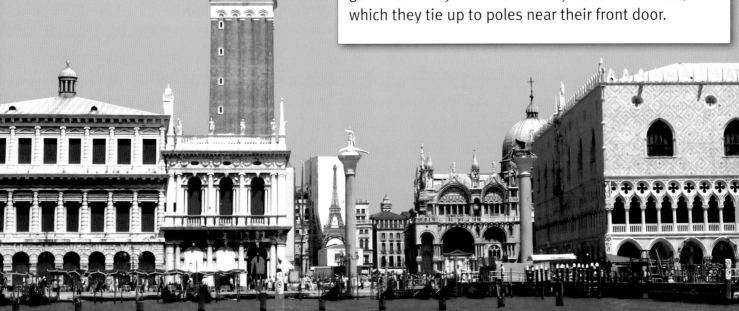

Bridges, Bridges and More Bridges

Most cities are made up of 'blocks'. Each block is an area, often square, with a road running along each side. In Venice the blocks have many different shapes and have canals running along each side. Each block is an island. Venice is made up of more than 100 islands and, to save you from getting wet when moving from one island to another, there are over 400 bridges.

Pigeons, Pigeons and More Pigeons

St Mark's Square is in the centre of Venice. It is surrounded by beautiful old buildings and is the most popular area visited by tourists. It is also the most popular area for visiting pigeons. About 10,000 pigeons visit the square each day, attracted by tourists, who buy small bags of corn to feed them.

Hang Out Your Washing for All to See

In the warm sunny days of summer, locals hang their washing out to dry above the streets and canals. Many houses are brightly painted and have flower boxes at their windows.

Venice: Fast Facts

Country: Italy
Capital city: No
Urban population: 300,000
Language: Italian
Money: Euro

Great for Over 2000 Years

ATHENS

People have been living in Athens for nearly 3500 years, making it one of the oldest continuously inhabited places on earth. It is often referred to as the 'birthplace of democracy' because of its early development of a form of government where people voted to elect their leaders. Democratic government was first used about 2500 years ago.

Ancient Athens

Athens was the most powerful city in the western world between 500 and 320 BCE, but it is not the military and naval power that people remember it for. The city is remembered for its wonderful buildings, temples and sculptures. Many of these great works were made during an ancient period of military strength. The city was rich and a safe place for artists to work.

Modern Athens

Athens hosted the first modern Olympic Games in 1896 and again in 2004. The Olympic city has all the features of other modern cities with tall buildings, busy shops and crowded streets. It's a perfect place to live if you want to explore ancient history.

Athens:
Fast Facts

Country: Greece
Capital city: Yes
Urban population: 4,000,000
Language: Greek
Money: Euro

ROME

Rome has the wonderful St Peter's Basilica that can hold 60,000 people. It has all those ancient Roman ruins, such as the Colosseum and the Pantheon, and then it has all those fashion shops and gelato stalls. Yes, Rome is a great city.

City of Fountains

Rome has many fountains. This one, the Trevi Fountain, is the best known. It is said that you will return to Rome if you throw coins into it. Many people seem to believe this. About 3000 euros are thrown into the fountain every day. How much is a euro worth in our money?

Ancient Rome

Rome was the most powerful city in the world in the period roughly 300 years before and after the birth of Christ. Its armies conquered the lands surrounding the Mediterranean Sea, much of Western Europe and Britain and brought enormous wealth back to Rome. With its riches, various emperors were able to build entertainment centres such as the Colosseum, temples to their many gods and monuments to their successes. The remains of some of these can still be seen today.

It Started as a Gaol
SYDNEY

Because its laws were so strict, England's gaols of the 1780s were full to overflowing. How could it reduce the number of prisoners? In 1787 a fleet of 11 ships with a cargo of convicts, soldiers, sailors, supplies and equipment sailed from England. On 26 February 1788 they reached Sydney Harbour. There were 543 male convicts, 189 female convicts and 18 children of convicts. This day is remembered as 'Australia Day'.

Designed and Built by Convicts

The first convicts lived in tents. During the day they built roads, made bricks and constructed permanent buildings. Many of them had been transported to Australia for committing minor crimes such as stealing a loaf of bread. Others were much more dangerous and required locking up at night. The Hyde Park Barracks, lived in by both soldiers and convicts, were designed and built by convicts. Today, you don't have to be a convict to go in and have a look.

A Bridge was Needed

As more people arrived, Sydney grew rapidly and spread along the southern side of the harbour. Settlement on the north side was slower as it required a boat ride, long walk or drive to get there. In 1932 a bridge was built across the harbour. It carries eight lanes of motor traffic, two rail lines, a cycle path and a pedestrian way. If you're feeling brave, you can walk to the very top of the arch.

How About Some Fun?

Behind this smiling face is central Sydney's largest amusement park. Built in 1935, it's nearly as old as the Harbour Bridge and sits on the waterfront land used during the bridge's construction. Entry is free. You do have to pay for the rides though.

Beaches, Beaches, Beaches

Sydney is famous for its beautiful beaches. It has around 50 of them that open onto the Tasman Sea, plus others around Botany Bay and along the harbour shore. In summer, people flock to these beaches to swim, surf, play volleyball and other sports, or just lie around on the warm golden sand. Would you like to build a sand castle on this beach and then try to keep the waves from washing it away? This is Bondi, Australia's most famous beach. It's just 7 kilometres from the centre of the city.

Where Has the River Gone?

A small river called the Tank Stream provided freshwater for the first settlement. The early convicts and settlers built houses close to this water supply. It ran down into Sydney Harbour between what is now the Opera House and the Harbour Bridge. Today, no part of the river can be seen—it runs beneath buildings and roads.

Sydney:
Fast Facts

Country: Australia
Capital city: state of NSW
Urban population 4,000,000
Language: English
Money: Aus dollar

The Old and New
Cuzco

Its Rise, Fall and Rise Again

Cuzco was the capital city of the Incas. The Incas ruled a large empire until defeated by the invading Spanish in 1533. The city declined under Spanish rule because it was no longer a capital. Only after the development of tourism as a major industry in the last 100 years has the city regained its importance. The major tourist attraction is the ancient Inca ruins.

Built on History

The Inca were great builders and when Cuzco was captured by the Spanish it already had many fine buildings. The Spanish, who were also famous builders, then built their own churches and palaces in their newly won city. Some of the building materials they used came from dismantling old Inca buildings. This Spanish Church of Santo Domingo sits on the ruins of an Inca sun temple. All the lower stone walls of the church are from the old Inca building.

Cuzco:
Fast Facts

Country: Peru
Capital city: No, but was until 1533
Urban population: 400,000
Language: Spanish
Money: Nuevo sol

The Ruins

Many people pass through Cuzco on their way to visit the Inca ruins at Machu Pichu. These ruins are considered to be one of the 'Seven Modern Wonders' of the world by many people. Tourists visit this site to wonder at the building skills of the Inca.

Rio de Janeiro

A New Year's Mistake

The city's site was discovered on 1 January 1502. The discoverer thought that the bay on which Rio de Janeiro is sited was the mouth of a large river and hence named it Rio de Janeiro – which means River of January.

A Ride to the Top

Sugarloaf Mountain rises straight up from within the city. The mountain is a large granite dome, stands 396 metres (1300 feet) high and the top can be reached by cable car.

Let's Have a Party!

Copacabana (Copa- ca-bana) Beach is one of the world's great beaches. Its 4-kilometre (2½-mile) long stretch of sand forms the centrepiece of Rio's party scene. Every New Year's Eve two million people come to the beach for parties. Copacabana is used for more than parties though. Volleyball, a variety of water sports, sun-baking and dancing are all popular. The World Beach Soccer Championships are held at Copacabana Beach most years.

Rio de Janeiro: Fast Facts

Country: Brazil
Capital city: No, but was until 1960
Urban population: 12,000,000
Language: Portuguese
Money: Real

Capitals Past and Present
KYOTO

Kyoto became capital of Japan in 794, when the emperor of that time decided that it was the right place to build his palace. In 1868 the capital was changed to Tokyo. You visit Kyoto to look at its temples, gardens, shrines, old buildings and its culture. It's not a place to drive around — it's a place to walk.

No Shortage of Places to Pray

There are more than 1600 temples in Kyoto. Most are built of wood and are brightly painted. The Golden Temple was built in 1397 but burned down in 1950. It was rebuilt in 1955. The upper two levels are coated with pure gold, but don't think you can steal it. The gold is only a 2000th of a mm thick. That makes it much thinner than a coat of paint.

Japanese Gardens

Traditional Japanese gardens probably don't look like the garden at your home. They are often very simple and do not contain masses of flowers. Rather, they rely on their patterns of rocks, sand and shrubs for their beauty.

Kyoto Streets

Away from the main shopping areas, some of the old streets are narrow and may even have stairs. You may even see some women wearing traditional clothing. Older houses are built of wood, and furniture is simple with traditional bed being mats on the floor. Would you like to sleep in a traditional Japanese bed?

Kyoto: Fast Facts

Country: Japan
Capital city: No, but was until 1868
Urban population: 1,500,000
Language: Japanese
Money: Yen

CANBERRA

When the Australian colonies unified to form an independent country in 1901, Canberra did not exist. It was a sheep paddock. It was decided to build a new capital city somewhere between the country's two largest cities, Melbourne and Sydney. In 1911 an international competition was held to design the city and an American architect, Walter Burley Griffin, was the winner.

A Temporary Building That Became Permanent

The first Parliament House opened in 1927 as a 'temporary' building to serve until a 'proper' one could be built. New Parliament House opened in 1988. It is unusual because it has been built into the top of a hill. Much of its roof is covered by lawns, but mowers are used to cut the grass now rather than the sheep that would have done it in the early days.

Everything is Modern

The buildings in Canberra are modern and the streets are wide. The city centre is surrounded by a green belt of nature parks, sporting fields and a lake. Strict planning laws ensure that most people live outside the green belt in suburbs. Expressways link the suburbs to the city centre. If you want to explore Canberra you need wheels—a bike, a car or a bus.

The Christmas Carol City
PRAGUE

Do you know the Christmas Carol:
> **Good King Wenceslas looked out**
> **On the feast of Stephen**
> **When the snow lay round about**
> **Deep and crisp and even?**

You do? That's good. Well, King Wenceslas was in Prague when he was looking out. Prague was where he lived.

The King of the Castle

Good King Wenceslas died more than 1000 years ago but over that time Prague Castle has grown to become the largest castle in the world. Various palaces and other building have been added by later kings and queens. The castle complex now contains four separate palaces, four large entertaining halls, two churches and eight other main buildings. The guards at the castle gates are changed every hour.

The Bridge Between the Castle and the City

A bridge over the Vltava River allows people to walk from the castle on one side of the river to Prague's main shopping area on the other side. In the past it was the only bridge over the river, but now there are many other bridges. It is used by pedestrians only. Buskers, artists and sellers of trinkets line the bridge, hoping to make some money from the passing tourists.

Something Different

Many European cities have lots of museums, galleries and theatres. Prague has all of these, but, in addition, it has something special. It has a puppet theatre. You can go to this theatre and watch performances of puppets and music that last for over an hour.

Not an Ordinary Clock

You could not put this clock in your house. It's nearly as big as a house. Prague's astronomical clock is built into the city's town hall. The original clock was made in 1410. That makes it 600 years old. The moving statues on the sides of the clock and the calendar were added in the 1800s. The clock tells the time, the seasons, the length of day, and the position of the earth, moon, sun and stars.

No Easter Bunny

In Prague they have real Easter eggs, not chocolate ones. It is traditional for girls and boys to paint patterns on real eggs and to exchange them on the Monday after Easter Day. If you don't have enough time to make a painted Easter egg you can buy one in a shop. Some of the prettiest eggs are works of art. If you are careful, you could try to paint an Easter egg yourself.

Prague:
Fast Facts

Country: Czech Republic
Capital city: Yes
Urban population: 2,000,000
Language: Czech
Money: Koruna

Russia's Jewel

ST PETERSBURG

Often old cities are dull and boring, but not St Petersburg. The tsars (kings) and tsarinas (queens) who ruled Russia from this capital city between 1712 and 1918 liked bright colours. Their many palaces were painted in blue and white, green and white or yellow and white.

What's in a Name?

Peter 'the Great' founded St Petersburg in 1703 and named the city not after himself, but after St Peter the Christian Apostle. The city's name was changed in 1914 to Petrograd, which in Russian translates to 'Peter's city'. Later, in 1924 it was changed to Leningrad after the famous Russian Revolutionary. Then in 1991 it was changed back to St Petersburg.

Peter, the Great Practical Joker

Peter the Great loved playing practical jokes. One of his favourites was to seat visitors around a fountain that was not working. When the guests were all in their chairs he would step away from the fountain and signal to a servant, who was hidden behind some bushes, to turn it on. The water would gush out, completely drenching everyone but Peter. Not very nice, but when you were tsar you could do whatever you liked.

Painted Ceilings

Not only were the palace walls brightly painted, so also were the ceilings. Artists had to lie on their backs on raised platforms to decorate the ceilings. The tsars were unbelievably rich. In many places where it looks as if gold paint was used, it wasn't paint, it was real gold.

Some Things are Very Modern

When you go to cross the street at a pedestrian crossing in St Petersburg you will notice that not only do you have a green 'walk' sign, but you also have a clock that tells you how much time you have left before the light goes red. That's a good idea, isn't it?

Magnificent Churches

Russian churches often have brightly coloured 'onion-shaped' domes on their roofs and walls made of coloured bricks and tiles. Some of the older churches were built by the tsars and tsarinas and are as beautiful on the inside as on the outside. This church (left) is St Isaac's.

St. Petersburg: *Fast Facts*

Country: Russia
Capital city: No, but was until 1918
Urban population: 5,000,000
Language: Russian
Money: Ruble

The Winter Palace and Hermitage

The most famous of the palaces is the Winter Palace. It was built by Peter the Great (he had a summer palace as well) and later was greatly enlarged by Tsarina Catherine the Great. Catherine's hobby was to collect art. She had an art gallery built onto one end of her palace to house her collection. She called her gallery 'The Hermitage' and it was bigger than the palace. Today, it is one of the world's greatest art galleries. The sculpture in the photo above is *The Crouching Boy* by the famous Italian artist Michelangelo.

The Shaky City
WELLINGTON

Wellington is the capital of the 'Shaky Isles', New Zealand. To be capital of the Shaky Isles you need to be shaky too—and Wellington is. It has small earthquakes so often that everyone who lives there is used to being shaken. If there was a large quake, many people could die or be injured.

Street Sculpture

All around the streets, you will see sculptures, like this silver globe. It is made up of ferns and hangs in the air in a city square. Can you see any other sculptures in these pictures of Wellington?

Are There Bees in There?

Not really, just people. This is Parliament, where politicians meet and public servants work to govern the country. We hope that they are as hard working as bees, but that's not what gives the building its nickname, 'The Beehive'. Can you guess why? Have a look at the shape of the building. Yes, it looks like a giant b.. h...

They All Fall Down

Because Wellington has so many earthquakes many of its older buildings, even multi-storied ones, were built of wood. Why wood? Because wood tends to bend and wobble during an earthquake, but doesn't fall down. If bricks had been used in the walls they would have cracked and if the earthquake was big enough, the buildings would have collapsed. Fortunately builders now use steel frames that work even better than wood.

The Festival City

Festivals are all the go in Wellington. They have festivals for arts, dance, food, Chinese new year, summer, winter, sport and just about anything else you can think of. Some you should not miss are those associated with Maori culture which feature dancing, cooking, wood carving, art, music, film making, face decorating, history and more.

It Looks Calm Today

But, on the night of 9 April 1968, a storm blew up with winds of 275 kilometres (170 miles) per hour, forcing the ferry *Wahine* onto a reef at the head of Wellington Harbour. Fifty-three people died. Wellington is often blasted by fierce winds blowing from Antarctica.

Wellington: Fast Facts

Country: New Zealand
Capital city: Yes
Urban population: 400,000
Languages: English, Maori and New Zealand sign language
Money: NZ dollar

Living and Shopping in the Medina

FES

Fes is a large city in northern Morocco on a fertile strip of land between the Atlantic Ocean and the Sahara Desert. The most interesting part of Fes is its medina, which is the old section of the city. It is a crowded place where manufacturing, shopping and housing are all crammed together in a great jumble.

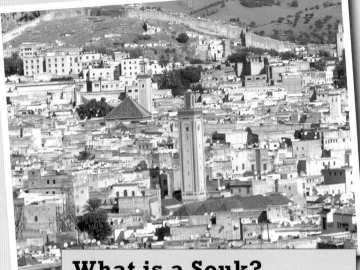

What is a Souk?

Although the medina is a jumble, it has particular parts that specialise in one or other activities. Each of these specialised areas is called a souk (pronounced 'sook'). For example, there is the leather souk, where leather is dyed (far left) and leather goods such as handbags and shoes are made (left) and where people who work in the leather industry live. People shopping in the souk always haggle over the price they have to pay for goods.

Keeping Your Cool in a Hot Souk

Summer temperatures in Fes are often over 40°C (104°F). To keep the non air-conditioned souks cool, the alleys are covered with slats or hessian. This allows the heat to rise through the covers and provides shades for those below.

No Trucks Here

Large packages are moved around the medina and its souks on donkeys. The alleys between buildings are too twisty and narrow for motor vehicles and, in some places, even for motorbikes and bicycles.

What Will We Eat Today?

Food shops are small—very small. Each specialises in a limited range of foods. You may go to two or three shops, buying one or two things from each, just to get your lunch. Eye-catching displays of the stallholder's food make it difficult to walk by without buying something. Can you see something you would like to eat?

The Entertainers

Musicians, dancers, jugglers, snake charmers and owners of animal acts arrive early each day to get the best places to perform in any open space in or near the medina.

Fes:
Fast Facts

Country: Morocco
Capital city: No, but was for long periods between 1269 and 1912
Urban population: 1,000,000
Language: Arabic
Money: Dirham

The Face of Modern China
SHANGHAI

Shanghai, with 17 million people, is one of the largest cities in the world. That's almost equal in population to that of the whole of Chile or Australia. It's the most modern city in China and it is through Shanghai that much of China's trade with the rest of the world is organised.

A Trading City from Long Ago

Many European countries began trading with China through the port of Shanghai in the years between 1840 and 1900. Along the river front, they constructed European-style buildings that became Shanghai's business centre. These buildings remain but the main business centre has moved to a new area on the other side of the river. The main goods traded in the 1800s were opium, silk and tea.

From Swamp to Skyscrapers

In 1990 a decision was made to build a new modern business district on swamp and farmland on the opposite side of the river to the older established city. All the buildings you see in this photo have been built in less than 20 years.

In A Hurry? Take the Train

It usually takes about an hour to travel from the airport to central Shanghai by taxi. If you want to get there quickly, take the new Maglev train. At speeds of up to 430 kilometres (270 miles) per hour, it takes just eight minutes to do the same trip.

Shopping

Nanjing Road is one of the busiest shopping streets in the world. More than a million people — workers, shoppers and tourists — walk along this street every day. Most shops are open late every night until around 10 p.m. That is still not enough time to go into all the shops in one day. This street is over 5 kilometres (3 miles) long.

Modern Trade

What do all the people who live in this big city do?
Many work in shops and offices, drive buses and cars or they may be teachers or nurses. Most, however, work in factories, making things such as clothing, steel, cars and chemical products. These products are sold throughout China and the rest of the world.

The Old City

You can still see traces of the old Shanghai—like this traditional boat—in the modern city. In the last few decades lots of people have moved here from farming areas where wages are lower and jobs harder to find.

I Live in the Apartment With a Red Roof

Nearly everyone in Shanghai lives in an apartment—and, as in other world cities, many apartment buildings look the same. When you tell your friends to come and visit it's no use just saying 'the one with the red roof' — you need to tell them the street name and number, the floor number and the apartment number or they will never find you.

Shanghai: Fast Facts

Country: China
Capital city: No
Urban population: 17,000,000
Language: Chinese Mandarin
Money: (Renminbi) Yuan

Ancient China

LIJIANG

More than six million people visit Lijiang every year. More than five million of these come for one reason only — to visit the old city. Lijiang is in southwestern China, near the border with Tibet.

Old Town, Old Ways

The married woman with the blue apron is wearing traditional clothes. We know that she is married because her apron is blue. Single women wear white aprons and grandmothers wear black ones. The woman is also carrying a back basket because she is going shopping. She will use the basket to carry the groceries back home.

What Will We Eat for Dinner?

The Chinese eat a wide variety of foods, some of which are quite different from western food. They eat lots of rice and vegetables mixed with fish, chicken, pork or beef. They also eat some insects. How would you like some fried crickets with crunchy bread, as in this photo?

Colourful Clothing

Every night in Lijiang, groups of local people perform their traditional dances for tourists. The dancing is very colourful and fast moving. Female dances are usually romantic and the male dances often include acrobats or fighting with traditional-style swords and wooden poles.

Shops, Shops and More Shops

So many tourists come to the old part of Lijiang that the ground floors of most of the two-storey buildings are used for shops. Some of the goods sold are touristy trinkets and souvenirs, others sell clothing and food. There are lots of restaurants. Most of the people live in apartments above the shops.

Bridges

The city is kept clean by three small rivers that run through it. Rubbish that finds its way into the streams is carried away by the flowing water. The water is surprisingly clean and lots of goldfish can be seen swimming in the rivers. To get into many houses or shops you have to cross small stone or wooden bridges.

Old and the New

Lijiang has grown quickly in the last 30 years and a new city has grown outside the old one. If you look closely at this photo you can see where the old city finishes and the new one begins. The old city is low and grey, and the new has taller buildings and wider streets. Can you see the difference?

No Cars, Trucks or Buses Here

Because the streets of the old city are so narrow and windy— and some even have stairs— deliveries are made using back baskets or by bicycle. This man is delivering bottles of drinking water to a restaurant.

Lijiang: *Fast Facts*

Country: China
Capital city: No
Urban population 1,200,000
Language: Chinese
Money: (Rinminbi) Yuan

Surrounded by a Wall
ROTHENBURG

Rothenburg still looks much the same as it did 600 years ago. Surrounded by a wall, its buildings are very, very old, and its cobblestone streets are narrow and twisty. What's new? Houses have electricity, cars drive along some of the wider streets and there are lots of shops and tourists.

People Believed in Witches

When Rothenburg was first built, the people who lived there believed in witches. Not all witches were thought to be bad. Some were good. Today, if you sit in the corner of a restaurant in the city you will have a good witch looking over your shoulder checking to see that you eat all your vegetables.

The City Wall

The stone wall that circles the ancient city is 3.4 kilometres (2.1 miles) long. On the inside, the wall had stairs that led up to a covered walkway. It goes all the way round the wall, making it possible for you to walk the same route taken by soldiers who fought battles from here hundreds of years ago.

Then Cannons were Invented

When cannons started to be used in warfare, a fort was added to the wall at the main southern entrance. The rooms in the fort are large enough for horses to have been used to move the cannons and to bring ammunition and gunpowder to the soldiers operating the large guns.

Gateways

There are six main gateways into the old city. Most gateway buildings were as large as this. They were where the soldiers slept and had their meals. One gateway, however, is quite different. It passes through the end of a church, which was built into the wall, and there is a home above the gate.

Getting Around

Cars are banned from driving in the city centre in the middle of the day and for most of the weekend. If you are too tired to walk at these times, you can still hire a horse and carriage to take you round the streets.

Rothenburg: *Fast Facts*

Country: Germany
Capital city: No
Urban population: 12,000
Language: German
Money: Euro

The Holy City
JERUSALEM

Jerusalem is one of the world's oldest cities, having first been settled more than 5000 years ago. It is a holy city for three of the world's great religions: Judaism, Christianity and Islam. Often referred to as the 'City of Peace', Jerusalem does not live up to its name. It has been attacked 75 times, and even today occasional fighting occurs between the Israelis (Jews) and the Palestinians (Muslims) who live there.

Israel's Parliament

Israel's parliament is called the Knesset. Members of the Knesset are elected for four years by all Israeli citizens aged 18 and over. A permanent Knesset building was built in 1966.

2000 Years of History

Christians have held church services on the site of Jesus's burial place (a sepulchre) for nearly 2000 years. The Roman emperor, Constantine the Great, began building a large domed church, the Church of the Holy Sepulchre (right), on the site in the year 326. This was destroyed in 1009 but partly rebuilt 40 years later.

Be Sure to Bring a Hat

To followers of the Jewish faith, the Western Wall is one of the holiest of sites. The wall was built only 20 years before the birth of Christ to surround a Jewish temple. The wall is the oldest remaining part of the ancient temple complex. If you visit the site you must wear a hat. If you have forgotten to bring one, free ones are available at the entrance.

Shopping for a Present

If you want to buy presents in Jerusalem, go straight to the bazaar, or market area. Some shops in the bazaar specialise in selling gifts such as copperware, jewellery or rugs and others seem to sell everything. If you went to this shop, you would find many different things to buy.

Getting Instructions on How to Live

In the year 621, Muhammad the founder of the Islamic religion, is said to have had a dream in which he went from his home in Mecca to the Temple area of Jerusalem and then onto Heaven, where he met Allah (God). At this meeting Allah instructed Muhammad that his followers should pray five times a day. The Dome of the Rock was built on the site of an old Jewish temple. It is the oldest Muslim building in the world.

Jerusalem: *Fast Facts*

Country:
Israel/Palestine
Capital city: Yes
Urban population:
800,000
Language:
Hebrew/Arabic
Money: Shekel

The Trading City
SINGAPORE

Singapore is more than a city—it's a country. It's also a young city, founded in 1819 by the British as a trading port on a small island near Malaysia. It's still a city built on trade, but now it's a big modern city governed by the people who live there, free from the control of a foreign country.

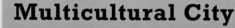

Multicultural City

Although the largest racial group is Chinese, there are large numbers of Malays, Indians and Europeans in the city. Most people can speak Chinese and English and most Indians also speak their own language.

Merlion, the Fish With a Lion's Head

Merlion, an imaginary animal with the body of a fish and the head of a lion, is a symbol of Singapore. Merlion is made from two words 'mer' and 'lion'. 'Mer' in the Malay language means 'sea' and 'lion', of course, is an animal. The original name of Singapore was 'Singapura' which means 'lion city'.

Tourists and More Tourists

Tourists flock to Singapore for two reasons: the shopping and the year-round warm days. You can buy almost anything in Singapore. If you are good at bargaining, you can buy most things even cheaper than in the countries where they are made. Tourists stay in modern resort hotels where they can lie around the pool in temperatures of around 30°C (86°F) every day of the year.

Shop Till You Drop!

You have probably heard the expression 'you can shop till you drop'. It's true in Singapore. There are shops everywhere selling clothing, toys (you'd like that), electronic gadgets, furniture and lots more. Shops come in all shapes and sizes, from people selling watches on the street and food from small portable barrows through to gigantic shopping malls.

Living in Apartments

Nearly four and a half million people live on Singapore Island and so there is not enough land for people to live in single houses surrounded by gardens. Nearly everyone lives in tall apartment buildings.

Singapore: *Fast Facts*

Country: Singapore
Capital city: Yes
Urban population: 4,500,000
Language: English/ Chinese/Malay/Tamil
Money: Singapore dollar

Living Near the Arctic Circle
TRONDHEIM

The name 'Trondheim' is made from two words: 'trond', meaning a good place, and 'heim', meaning home, so Trondheim is a good place to have your home. The people who live here are fishermen, shopkeepers, traders, ordinary working people and university students. The city began as a Viking settlement in 997 and was Norway's capital until 1217.

'I Don't Want to Go to Bed! The Sun's Still Up!'

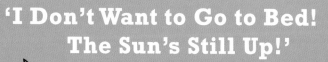

Trondheim is quite close to the Arctic Circle. In summer it has very long days, and in winter the nights are very, very long. In midsummer, the sun rises at around two o'clock in the morning and sets about 11 pm at night. Even when the sun is down, there is plenty of light. There is no darkness between 20 May and 20 July each year. In midwinter, the sun peeps over the horizon for just three hours each day.

Even the Palace is Made of Wood

The Royal Palace, used by the king and queen when they visit Trondheim, is built entirely of wood. There is no fence around the palace and the front door opens directly onto the street.

Beware of Fire!

Trondheim is surrounded by forests and so nearly all buildings are built from wood. When there are wild fires in this region, it's not the forests that burn, it's the houses. The fires spread rapidly from one building to another. The city has been burned ten times in its 1000-year history. In rebuilding the city after the 1681 fire, streets were widened to reduce the chance of fire spreading from one side of the street to another. The city still has wide streets and large market squares.

A Busy Waterfront

Trondheim is at the head of a 130-kilometre (80-mile) long fiord. Large, colourful old wooden warehouses along the shore are used to store goods that arrive at the city by boat. Fish, timber, animal furs (in the old days) and farm produce are also stored in the warehouses waiting to be shipped out.

Trolls

Trolls are mythical creatures that supposedly lived in the dark forests of Norway. They also lived under waterfalls, in caves and other dark places. Some were good and others bad. If they came out into the light they were turned solid. They had long noses, four fingers on each hand and four toes on each foot. This troll must have been caught on the rock just as the sun rose.

Trondheim:
Fast Facts

Country: Norway
Capital city: No, but was until 1217
Urban population: 200,000
Language: Norwegian
Money: Norwegian krone

Stone Buildings Burn Too

The cathedral, built in 1070, is one of the few buildings in the city made of stone. It has burned down four times. How does a stone building catch on fire? Through its roof. The roof is made of wooden rafters covered by wooden shingles. Norway's kings and queens are always crowned in the cathedral and the royal jewels are kept here.

Too Tired for the Steep Hill?

Trondheim has an unusual bicycle lift—like a ski tow, but it is set in the roadway. You can use the tow to take your bike to the top of a steep hill.

ACTIVITIES

THE WORLD CITIES QUIZ

1. Why are there so many pigeons in Venice? (page 17)

2. What does the name 'Rio de Janeiro' mean? (page 23)

3. What do the letters UN stand for? (page 10)

4. On what river is Paris located? (page 14)

5. In which two years were the modern Olympic Games held in Athens? (page 18)

6. From where did the Spanish get some of the stone they used to build churches in Cuzco? (page 22)

7. For how many years was Australia's temporary Parliament House used before it was replaced by a new one? (page 25)

8. Which of the cities mentioned in this book has the largest population? (You will have to look in the Fast Facts boxes to find the answer.)

9. Why don't you find cars and trucks in the streets of Venice? (page 16)

10. What is a 'Merlion'? (page 42)

11. On what street will you find the New York Stock Exchange? (page 10)

12. What is the correct name for the clock in the tower attached to London's Parliament House? (page 12)

13. How many palaces are there in Prague's Castle? (page 26)

14. For how many years was Kyoto capital of Japan? (page 24)

15. Why was wood used to construct many of Wellington's buildings? (page 31)

16. What speed does Shanghai's Magleve train travel at? (page 34)

THINGS TO DO

1. Ask Mum or Dad to hardboil an egg for you, then colour it to make a Prague-style Easter egg.

2. Write a letter to a friend telling them how— as a soldier or a nurse—you helped defend Rothenburg from an army equipped with battering rams, spears and arrows.

3. Make a list of ten cities you would most like to visit (they don't have to be the same as the ones in this book) and then write two or three lines about what you would hope to see and do in each.

4. With a friend, pretend that you are haggling to buy a gift at a small shop in the centre of Fes. One of you can be the buyer and the other the shop owner.

GLOSSARY

Astronomical clock A clock that tells the time of day and also shows more information such the positions of the moon, planets, sun and stars.

BCE Before the Christian Era—that is, before the birth of Christ.

Barracks A place where soldiers, police or convicts live.

Basilica A large church.

Battering ram An attacking weapon used by soldiers to knock down walls and gates. The simplest was a wooden log carried by several attackers, who ran and pounded the end of the log as hard as they could against their target.

Bazaar A market place in Western Asia, the Middle East or North Africa that has many small shops selling a wide variety of goods crowded into a small area.

Buskers Singers, musicians, jugglers and other artists who perform in front of a crowd hoping that the people will be entertained and in reward will give them some money.

CE In the Christian era, that is, after the birth of Christ.

Colonies Countries claimed and controlled by another and more powerful country.

Convict A person convicted of a crime who is serving a goal sentence.

Culture The traditions and way of life of people.

Democratic government A type of government where people vote to elect their representatives.

Fiord A U-shaped glacial valley that runs down to the sea.

Granite A very hard rock that has cooled from a molten state many kilometres below the earth's surface.

Haggle To bargain when buying goods.

Maglev A type of very fast train that relies on magnets to hold it above its rails and to make it move forward.

Middle East Countries at the eastern end of the Mediterranean Sea, including Egypt, Israel, Palestine, Lebanon, Iraq, Syria and Iran.

Medina The old centre of North African and Middle East cities.

Observatory A scientific building from where astronomers can study the stars.

Rafters Large wooden planks used to hold up a building's roof.

Shingles Thin plates of wood that are laid like tiles to form the roof of a building to keep out rain and snow.

Shrine A place or object of worship.

Snake charmers Entertainers who use music to make snakes gently move and sway.

Souk A specialised part of a medina where the people who live there work in the same industry.

Tsar The Russian emperor or king.

Tsarina The Russian empress or queen.

Warehouses Building where goods are stored.

WANT TO KNOW MORE?

BOOKS

All general encyclopedias, such as *Americana*, *Britannica*, *Compton's* and *World Book*, have entries for individual cities. They are good sources of information, not only for cities mentioned in this book, but for many other cities you may be interested in researching.

Travel guides can also be an excellent resource for information on cities.

WEBSITES

There are thousands of websites for cities, far too many to list here. If you wish to research a particular city, put the name of the city into your computer's search engine, together with another word such as 'kids' or 'history' or 'geography' or 'sites' and see what comes up.

If you don't add the second word you will get lots of advertisements for hotels and accommodation.If you are experienced at using a computer, you may be able to use one or more of the online encyclopedias such as *Britannica*, *Encarta*, *World Book* or *Wikipedia*.

INDEX